CLEAN WATER for ELIROSE

Ariah Fine

Illustrated by Don Robb

FOR BRETON AND ADYRA

May your hearts flow with compassion.

Illustrator: Don Robb
Cover and Interior Design: Keane Fine
First Printing 2010
Printed in the United States of America

ISBN 13: 978-1-4414-2277-4
ISBN 10: 1-4414-2277-3

CreateSpace   18 17 16 15 14 13 12 11 10
13   12   11   10   9   8   7   6   5   4   3   2   1

CLEAN WATER for ELIROSE

Ariah Fine

Illustrated by Don Robb

What do you like to drink? Pop? Water? Milk? Juice? Do you like it if your drink is dirty and yucky? Me neither. My name is Maria. I like to drink orange pop when my parents take me out to eat at a restaurant. I get to order from a big menu. My pop is fizzy and delicious.

This is my friend, Joey. He gets soda pop all the time. He has some in his cupboard, so he can have it whenever he wants. Joey likes how sweet tasting the soda pop is.

Tasha is my friend too. She doesn't drink soda pop because her parents say it's bad for her teeth. She drinks juice instead. Tasha loves fruit and fruity drinks.

Derrick is Tasha's older brother. He doesn't like juice or pop, he likes to drink bottled water. Derrick's water is clean and tasty.

This is Elirose; she lives in Haiti. She never gets to drink pop or juice. She has to walk a long way every day to get water for her family. And the water isn't even clean, it's yucky and dirty. I didn't know that there were kids just like you and me who don't even have clean water to drink!

Joey, Tasha and I wanted to help Elirose. We asked Tasha's dad how we could help. He said that if Elirose's village had a well they could have clean water to drink right near their homes. A well is a deep hole in the ground that fills with water. We decided we should do something to help Elirose build a well. But how could we help?

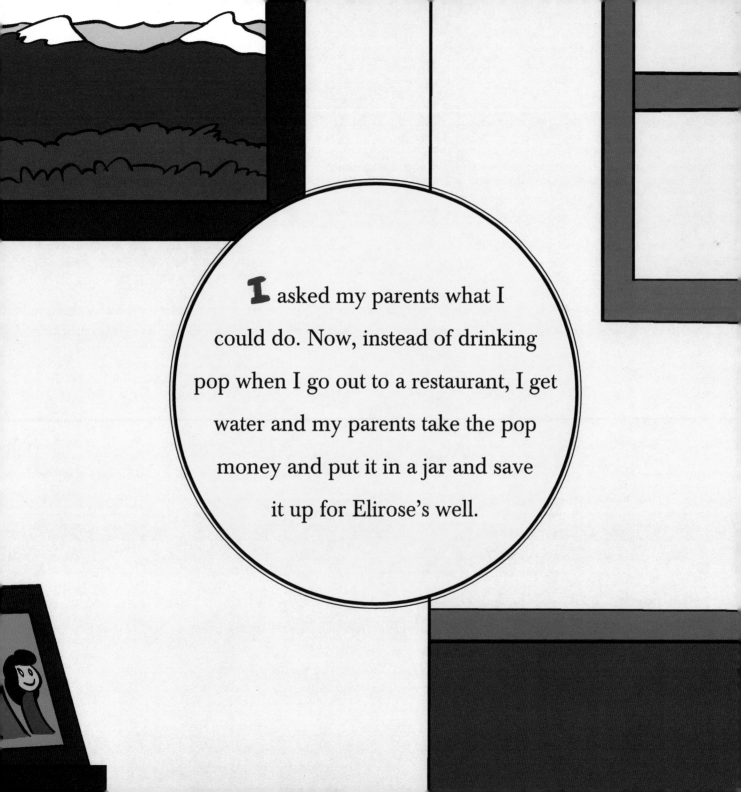

I asked my parents what I could do. Now, instead of drinking pop when I go out to a restaurant, I get water and my parents take the pop money and put it in a jar and save it up for Elirose's well.

Joey asked the people in his community to donate money to help Elirose build a well.

Tasha and her brother Derrick used their allowance to set up a lemonade stand in their neighborhood. They took all the money they made selling lemonade and gave it to Elirose's village to build a well.

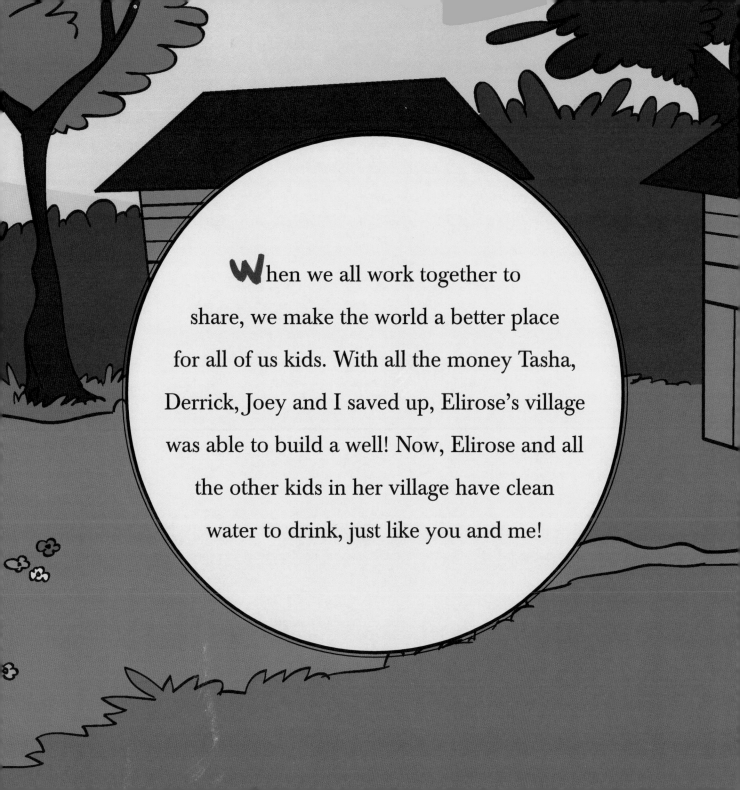

When we all work together to share, we make the world a better place for all of us kids. With all the money Tasha, Derrick, Joey and I saved up, Elirose's village was able to build a well! Now, Elirose and all the other kids in her village have clean water to drink, just like you and me!

DISCUSSION QUESTIONS

For your family or classroom

- Have you ever had to eat or drink something that didn't taste good? Have you ever gotten sick from eating or drinking something? What was it and how did it make you feel?

- Can you imagine if you couldn't play or go to school because your family needed your help to get water to drink or grow food? How would that make you feel?

- What are the ways you could help these kids?

ACTIVITIES / IDEAS

MATH: Host your own fundraiser where your children give up something (special drinks or snacks) and you donate the cost difference to a water-related charity. Or have the kids do extra chores to earn donation money.

MATH: Have students run a lemonade stand or a car wash. Collect pennies or soda cans.

WRITING: Write letters or schedule speaking opportunities for students to talk about what they've learned and to encourage adults they know to donate.

WRITING: Choose a Student of The Week to feature: how can they/ did they make a difference in the life of another child? Have their parents help them write/illustrate what they did/will do and share it with the class.

WRITING: Write about how you would feel if you didn't have fresh water to drink.

SCIENCE: Design/write about a machine that would change dirty water into fresh water.

CLEAN WATER ORGANIZATIONS

CHARITY:WATER - http://www.charitywater.org

BLOOD:WATER MISSION - http://www.bloodwatermission.com

HAITI WATER PROJECT - http://www.haitiwaterproject.com

Made in the USA
Charleston, SC
05 October 2010